BENELUX RAILWAYS

John Law

First published 2017

Amberley Publishing
The Hill, Stroud
Gloucestershire, GL5 4EP

www.amberley-books.com

Copyright © John Law, 2017

The right of John Law to be identified as the Author of this work has been asserted in accordance with the Copyrights, Designs and Patents Act 1988.

ISBN 978 1 4456 6812 3 (print)
ISBN 978 1 4456 6813 0 (ebook)

All rights reserved. No part of this book may be reprinted or reproduced or utilised in any form or by any electronic, mechanical or other means, now known or hereafter invented, including photocopying and recording, or in any information storage or retrieval system, without the permission in writing from the Publishers.

British Library Cataloguing in Publication Data.
A catalogue record for this book is available from the British Library.

Origination by Amberley Publishing.
Printed in the UK.

Introduction

Belgium, the Netherlands and Luxembourg have long been linked together economically and the three countries' railways have followed suit. Nevertheless, each country and each railway system has its own peculiarities, making the Benelux area to be quite fascinating for any rail enthusiast like myself. I have been visiting the area since the early 1970s and the best of my photographic efforts is presented here, supplemented by a few shots from my old friend Tony Martens, who was born in Belgium, as well as from Richard Huggins, plus one from Erwin Voorhaar in the Netherlands. Thanks also to Anne Greenhalgh, Nicolas Pike and Erwin Voorhaar for a few lines of translation.

The Netherlands consists of twelve provinces, only two of which are called Holland, so the use of that term to describe the whole country is incorrect, even though a lot of the Dutch use it. Throughout the country the language is Nederlands (Dutch), except for the province of Friesland, where West Friesian may be encountered. English is widely spoken, though not so much in the northern provinces.

Most of the railway operations in the Netherlands are operated by Nederlandse Spoorwegen (NS), though private operators such as Syntus run a good number of the more rural services. Like much of Germany, right-hand running is the order of the day, making life very interesting at places like Roosendaal, where NS meets the Belgian rail network. Most of the network is electrified at 1.5Kv DC, though the newer lines such as the new high-speed route into Belgium use 25Kv AC overhead power. Many of the electric locos I encountered in the 1970s have since been withdrawn, including the famous ex-British Rail Co-Co class 77 once used on the Woodhead route.

As well as bordering Belgium, the Netherlands has one other international frontier, that with Germany. Regular services run between the two countries, with German ICE units regularly visiting Amsterdam. Various local services also cross the border, ranging from the Groningen to Leer service in the north, to the Heerlen–Aachen route out of Limburg province. Among other operators, Deutsche Bahn also runs many of the freight services in the Netherlands.

Like much of Europe, many of the cities and major cities of the Netherlands once had tram systems. Three still survive – Amsterdam, Rotterdam, and Den Haag (The Hague). Though this book does not look at traditional tramways, some of the operations of the Amsterdam Metro system are on street tracks so are included. Similarly, the Randstadrail network around Den Haag and the Utrecht *sneltram* are featured, as they are built to light rail standards using former NS rail routes. In addition, since 1968, Rotterdam has had its own metro system.

Like the Netherlands, Belgium is also divided in provinces – ten in all, plus Brussels. Five of those provinces speak a version of Dutch called Vlaams (Flemish), while the others form Wallonia, where French is spoken. Brussels is officially bilingual, where there is a small German-speaking area in Liège province, ceded to Belgium under the terms of the Treaty of Versailles in 1919. To add to the confusion, each town or city has names in both French and Dutch. Liège, for example, is Luik in Dutch (and Luttich in German!). We British do not help either, renaming Gent into Ghent and Antwerpen into Antwerp. Within these pages, the local names, in the correct language, will be used. Therefore, the city most Britons call Bruges will be referred to as Brugge, as it is in the Dutch-speaking province of West Vlanderen. The only exception to that rule is the country's capital (Brussel in Dutch/Bruxelles in French), where I will use 'Brussels' to prevent any bias towards either language.

The language differences extend to the railway network, with only the local language being used on stations and trains, except for Brussels. All internal trains are operated by the national railway company, Nationale Maatschappij der Belgische Spoorwegen (NMBS) in Dutch and Société Nationale des Chemins de Fer Belges (SNCB) in French. The appropriate abbreviation will be used throughout this book.

Unlike the Netherlands, left-hand running is the norm in Belgium and much of the rail system is electrified using a 3,000 volt DC overhead system. A mixture of multiple unit and loco-operated push-pull sets are used for the passenger services, with a few rush hour services in the hands of conventional loco-hauled trains. Freight services are provided by NMBS/SNCB, plus the national railways of France and Germany, along with several private operators.

The city of Brussels now has its own metro system, illustrated within, plus an extensive tram network, while both Antwerpen and Gent also have trams. Trams still operate on parts of the formerly nationwide Vicinal (French)/Buurtspoorweg (Dutch) metre gauge system, around Charleroi and along the entire Belgian coast. The Vicinal/Buurtspoorweg was a proper railway, often roadside, with both freight and passenger services and therefore it is appropriate that it is included in any book on Belgian railways.

The Grand Duchy of Luxembourg is much smaller than Belgium or the Netherlands. The official language here is French, but many people speak the local Luxembourgish. Despite its small size it has a cheap and reliable rail service, serving all parts of the country, including some internal journeys of over an hour (for example Luxembourg City to Troisvierges). A great variety of modern rolling stock is owned by the national rail operator Société Nationale des Chemins de Fer Luxembourgeois (CFL). Most lines are electrified. The city of Luxembourg itself has always been worth a visit for its main railway station has services operated not only by CFL but also the national operators of Belgium, Germany and France, plus coaching stock from other European Railways.

In conclusion, I hope you enjoy this book and that it inspires you to take a visit to all three countries and their fascinating rail systems.

Français

Merci d'avoir acheté mon livre *Benelux Railways* qui montre mes meilleurs photos prises en Belgique, Les Pays Bas et Luxembourg pendant mes visites fréquents depuis les années 1970. J'espère que vous aimerez ce livre.

John Law, Stevenage, Angleterre.

Nederlands

Welkom en bedankt voor het kopen van mijn boek *Spoorwegen in de Benelux-landen*, met de beste van mijn foto's in België, Nederland en Luxemburg welke ik tijdens frequente bezoeken, sinds de vroege jaren van de 1970 heb gemaakt. Ik hoop dat u ervan zal genieten!

John Law, Stevenage, Engeland.

The Netherlands

We start our tour of the Low Countries in the capital of the Netherlands, at the city's main railway station of Amsterdam Centraal, in 1972. Semaphore signalling was still in use there, as Nederlands Spoorwegen (NS) number 1212 sits under the fine signal gantry. In charge of a passenger train at the west end of the station, this classic electric locomotive was part of a batch of twenty-five similar engines built between 1951 and 1953. All had been withdrawn by 1998, but several were sold for further service to private operators and others went into preservation. Number 1211 is usually to be found in the railway museum in Utrecht.

Electrical multiple units (EMUs) like this were once common throughout the Netherlands' rail network. Seen at Amsterdam Centraal station in 1972, this yellow-liveried four-car 'Hondekop' (literally dog head) unit is about to depart westwards. Various versions of this basic but solid EMU type were delivered to NS from the early 1960s, in several lengths, for a multitude of passenger duties.

Another 'Hondekop' EMU, still in its old NS green colours, sits partly under the roof of Amsterdam Centraal station, again in 1972. Well situated for the tourist sights of the city, the station itself is well worth a visit. It was opened in its present form in 1889, designed by Pierre Kuypers, excluding the cast-iron roof that was built in sections in the United Kingdom, at Derby.

An example of a two-car 'Hondekop' EMU sits in Rotterdam Centraal station in 1972. Part of the 'Plan V' batch of units, this one would have been fairly new when photographed. At the time of writing, very few of this type remain in service. Rotterdam Centraal station has since undergone a major rebuild, the job finally being finished in 2014.

The Netherlands

Not all Nederlandse Spoorwegen electric locomotives were bought new. When British Rail closed the Manchester to Sheffield via Woodhead route to passengers, the EM2 (later known as Class 77) class of passenger locos became redundant. Consequently, all six were sold to NS in 1969 for further operation. One was scrapped for spares (BR number E27005), but the others became numbers 1501 to 1506. Number 1501 is seen here, at Rotterdam Centraal in 1976, on an express passenger service. In its BR times it had been E27003, named *Diana*. The loco has since been preserved in the Netherlands. Two further locos have been saved for posterity and have been returned to the UK.

Electrification of the railways of the Netherlands began in the 1930s, but is was not until the next decade that the need for electric locomotives was realised for coal, freight and long-distance passenger duties. Ten were ordered from Switzerland in 1942, but the war meant that SLM of Winterthur did not start delivery until 1947. Numbers 1001 to 1003 were built in Switzerland, but the rest of the batch – 1004-1010 – were constructed in the Netherlands by Werkspoor in Utrecht in 1949. The first of the Dutch-built batch, 1004, is seen at Roosendaal station, near the Belgian border, in November 1977. It was withdrawn in 1982 and scrapped, but the last of the batch was saved for preservation.

The Nederlandse Spoorwegen class 1100 electric locomotives were built by Alsthom in the 1950s, based on a French design. Never very popular with their drivers, the original angular-looking cabs were replaced by flat fronted versions, as seen on number 1113, one of the first to be so converted. It is seen on the evening boat train at Hoek van Holland Haven in late 1978, where connections were made with the ferry to Harwich, in England. The entire class had been withdrawn by the end of the twentieth century.

Nederlandse Spoorwegen also ordered a batch of sixteen six-axle electric locomotives from Alsthom, again similar to those of the French Railways. Delivery began in 1952 and continued until 1956. Most of the earlier locomotives were painted in a turquoise livery, but this was replaced by a dark blue colour scheme, as seen applied to number 1307 at Rotterdam Centraal in November 1977. In later years, standard NS yellow and grey paintwork was applied and each locomotive was named after a Dutch city, number 1307 becoming *Etten-Leur*. The last of the class was withdrawn in 2000, though four went into preservation.

The Netherlands

One of Nederlandse Spoorwegen's 1200 class of electric locomotive, number 1208, is seen on an international service calling at one of the country's most important railway stations, Utrecht Centraal, in 1978. At the time of writing, Utrecht Centraal station is nearing the end of a major rebuild.

Another member of the class, number 1205, is seen uncoupled from its train in November 1997, just after arriving at Roosendaal with a train from the Breda direction. Roosendaal is notable as it is the frontier interchange station between the Belgian and Netherlands rail systems, where the voltage changes from the Dutch 1.25 KV DC system to the Belgian 3,000 V DC overhead. It is also the point where the left-hand running of NMBS changes over to the opposite side for NS operation. Roosendaal is also the junction for the NS branch into Zeeland, as far as Vlissingen.

The Nederlandse Spoorwegen 600 class of locomotive will seem very familiar to British eyes. A total of sixty-five were built at English Electric in the early to mid-1950s and were very similar to British Rail's class 11 diesel shunters. NS number 638 is seen in the freight yard alongside Roosendaal station, where goods traffic was interchanged between the Dutch and Belgian railways. Today, the sidings are still used for the same purpose, but the wonderful collection of semaphore signals seen in this September 1983 picture is no more. The 600 class has since been withdrawn from the NS fleet, though several survive in private hands, in industrial use and in preservation.

In the mid- to late 1950s, 150 class 2200 diesel locomotives were built for Nederlandse Spoorwegen for freight and shunting duties. Until the 1970s, these carried NS maroon livery, but by the time of this photograph, November 1977, most had been painted in the grey and yellow colour scheme. Number 2289 and 2280 are seen coupled together in the yard at Roosendaal.

The Netherlands

We are again at Roosendaal in November 1977, where NS diesel-electric loco number 2526 is still in its old maroon colour scheme as it sits in the freight yard. Numerically one of the last members of the 2400 class, built by Alsthom between 1954 and 1957, with a maximum speed of 80 km/h, therefore mainly suited to freight traffic. All were withdrawn by 1991, though number 2498 resides in the museum in Utrecht.

In September 1983, two members of Nederlandse Spoorwegen's 2200 class, numbers 2340 and 2336 rest in a siding at Den Haag Hollands Spoor station. One of two principal stations in the city of Den Haag (correctly, 's-Gravenhage in Dutch, 'The Hague' in English), Hollands Spoor was opened in 1843, at the end of an extension of the oldest line in the country, from Amsterdam to Haarlem. In contrast to the terminal establishment at Den Haag Centraal, Hollands Spoor soon became a through station, served by the Rotterdam to Amsterdam route.

Another NS class 2400 locomotive, number 2462, is seen on an engineering train standing on one of the through tracks at Den Haag Hollands Spoor station in September 1983. The former passenger carriage behind the loco looks fascinating!

The Nederlandse Spoorwegen 'Mat '46' four-car electrical multiple units were introduced during the late 1940s and early 1950s. Therefore, when this particular set was photographed at Roosendaal in November 1977, it was decidedly ancient. Indeed, the first withdrawals of this class began in 1974 and all had gone by 1983. Two cars of one unit have been preserved and can occasionally be seen operating on the Dutch rail network.

The Netherlands

A Nederlandse Spoorwegen yellow-liveried four-car 'Hondekop' EMU rests in the sidings at Roosendaal station in November 1977. At the time semaphore signals were still controlling movements in the area. The signal box can be seen towering over the second car of the unit.

Seen from the adjacent yard of the preserved railway is a two-car NS 'Hondekop' EMU, standing in the station at Hoorn in September 1983. The unit has probably just terminated with a local service from the direction of Alkmaar. It will earlier have connected with an Amsterdam to Enkhuizen semi-fast service.

Ede is a small modern town in the Province of Gelderland. InterCity services call at Ede-Wageningen on the Utrecht to Arnhem route, but the heart of the town is served by Ede Centrum station on the single-track line from Amersfoort. Today, that line is served by modern 'Valleilijn' EMUs, but in June 1993 NS were in charge of operations, as a two-car 'Hondekop' EMU calls.

Emmen is another example of a modern Dutch town, in Drenthe Province, close to the German border. It is situated at the end of a double-track branch from Zwolle, where connections can be made for the rest of the country. On 23 June 2009, a Plan V 'Hondekop' four-car EMU has just terminated. Today the line is served by two trains an hour. At one time the line continued northwards, but closed in the 1950s.

The quiet village of Mariënberg, in Overijssel Province, is the location of a junction on the Zwolle to Emmen line, where a single-track branch from Almelo diverges. The hourly 'Stoptrein' service from Emmen departs on 23 June 2009, formed of a double set of two-car 'Hondekop' units.

Another pair of 'Hondekop' EMUs is seen at Roosendaal station forming a local service, on 8 October 2011. Sadly, the closest unit has been subject to 'tagging', something that afflicts many trains in the Netherlands. However, the Belgian Railways (NMBS) EMU, No. 823, on the left has also been attacked. Indeed, the problem tends to be worse in Belgium. No. 823 will form one of the hourly all stations service to Antwerpen Centraal.

Based on the 'Hondekop' Mat '64 passenger electrical multiple units, Nederlandse Spoorwegen ordered thirty-five single cars for postal duties, built by Werkspoor in the mid-1960s. Delivered new in a dull maroon colour scheme, they were later repainted as seen here in September 1983. Capable of hauling additional parcels cars, No. 3001 is standing in a siding at Den Haag Hollands Spoor station.

The first Nederlandse Spoorwegen 'Sprinter' EMUs were delivered in 1975 as two-car sets, such as this one seen at Rotterdam Centraal in 1978. Also known officially as 'Stadsgewestelijk Materieel' or 'Plan Y' by NS, the term 'Sprinter' was often applied to the sides of the units. Intended for stopping services, with fast acceleration, the original batch did not feature toilets, though the later ones did. Several sets were later strengthened to three-car and some of the last batch built was to that configuration. NS received the last units in 1983.

Nederlandse Spoorwegen's 'Sprinter' EMUs later received this smart yellow, white and blue livery, as seen applied to unit No. 2119 at Zutphen on 3 July 2010. Alongside is a diesel multiple unit set, forming a service to Apeldoorn. The town of Zutphen, in Gelderland, situated on the River IJssel, is an important junction on the Dutch Railway network.

Nederlandse Spoorwegen use two-car DMUs on the shuttle service between Zwolle and the delightful town of Kampen, though the railway station is sited on the opposite bank of the River IJssel. Built in the 1990s, these 'Buffel' (meaning 'buffalo' in Dutch) units are the only DMUs operated by NS at the time of writing. This one is seen in its bay platform at Zwolle, 23 June 2009.

Another two-car 'Buffel' DUM set sits in one of the through platforms at Zwolle on 12 October 2013. It is probably on some kind of test run as, apart from the Kampen branch, all lines out of Zwolle are electrified.

Nederlandse Spoorwegen had some earlier DMUs, mainly for rural lines in the north of the country. Known as the 'Wadlopers', one of the earlier DH1 single-car units is seen in a westbound facing bay platform at Leeuwarden, capital of the province of Friesland, around 2003. It will be heading to either Harlingen Haven or Stavoren. All 'Wadloper' sets had been withdrawn by 2008 and the services are now operated by Arriva.

The NS 1700 class electric locomotives are still to be found throughout the country, operating a variety of passenger duties, including push-pull double-deck trains. A total of eighty-one was built by Alsthom in the early 1990s. The class is similar, but with technical variants, from the earlier 1600 design. No. 1722 has just arrived on the rear of an express from Amsterdam at Lelystad on the first day of March in 2008. Lelystad is the capital of the newest Dutch Province, Flevoland, built on land reclaimed from the former Zuiderzee. Lelystad station was a terminal at the time, but the line has now been extended through to Zwolle, improving journey times to that location.

Sister locomotive No. 1757 is seen at the rear of a northbound InterCity express at Roosendaal on 24 June 2009. This will probably head east towards Breda and Arnhem.

Another NS class 1700 electric locomotive is seen at Amsterdam Centraal station on 5 May 2012. No. 1711 is in charge of a double-deck push-pull set, which it will propel eastwards out of the station.

On the same occasion of the above photograph, NS No. 1760 has just arrived at Amsterdam Centraal station, with an international express formed of Deutsche Bahn rolling stock. This train would have come from Germany via either Hengelo or Venlo, with the NS locomotive taking over from a DB one close to the border.

Though the prototype NS 'Koploper' electrical multiple units were introduced in 1977, the main batches were built by Talbot between 1983 and 1994. The name of the units derives from the Dutch for 'head walker', as it is possible for passengers to walk under the driving cabs when two sets are coupled together. Intended for long distance internal InterCity services, these trains are seen on most of the main lines in the country. Four-car unit No. 4068 is seen at Enkhuizen station – the terminus of the routes from Amsterdam via Hoorn – on 2 May 2012. The city of Enkhuizen, in Noord Holland province, is situated on what is left of the Zuiderzee, with summer ferry services to other former seaside towns.

One of the last 'Koploper' units to be built, No. 4247, is seen on a stopping duty, running from Utrecht to Leiden, running into the passing loop at Bodegraven on 4 May 2012. Bodegraven is a small, neat, middle-class town made famous in recent years for the excellent beers brewed here by Brouwerij de Molen.

The city of 's-Hertogenbosch, usually known as Den Bosch, is a fine place with lots of old architecture. In contrast, the modern financial building on the west side of the station, in the Paleiskwartier area, forms the backdrop to many photographs of NS trains here. One of the DD-IRM (full name Dubbeldeks InterRegio Materieel) four-car electric units stands in the station on 19 June 2009.

Two more DD-IRM units sit in the sidings at Roosendaal on 7 July 2010. These EMUs were introduced from 1994 onwards. Some were delivered as three-car sets, but most were four-cars. A recent programme has seen them being extended to six-car units to become VIRM (Verlengd InterRegio Materieel) sets.

Nederlandse Spoorwegen's other double-deck multiple units are the DD-AR class, consisting of a power car (with passengers on the upper deck only) and three bi-level trailers. The business end of one of these units is closest to the camera in this view at 's-Hertogenbosch station on 19 June 2009.

A recent modernisation programme has seen the rebuilding of the DD-AR multiple units to more modern standards, becoming the NID (Nieuwe Intercity Dubbeldeker) class. Here is an example, set number 7541, at Hoorn on 9 October 2013.

Beyond the ferry terminal at Hoek Van Holland Haven, the line continues for a few hundred yards to a terminus named Hoek Van Holland Strand (*Beach* in English). It is here that we see one of Nederlandse Spoorwegen's new 'Sprinter Lighttrain' EMU sets. Entering service in 2009, these units were meant to replace the earlier 'Hondekop' Mat '64 sets and are now commonplace on local duties in the western side of the Netherlands. Photographed on 5 July 2010.

Another NS 'Sprinter Lighttrain' is seen arriving at Amsterdam Centraal on 5 May 2012. This six-car set, No. 2605, has been operating a local service from the north of the capital.

The 'Hogesnelheidslijn Zuid' (HSL) – High Speed Line South in English – is a new construction from Amsterdam's Schipol Airport to the Belgian border, opened in 2009. It forms part of the 'Thalys' route from Paris and Brussels. With its branch to Breda (on the Roosendaal to Arnhem route), it was also intended to carry hourly 'Fyra' services to Brussels using these AnsaldoBreda built units. Unfortunately, they were so unreliable they were withdrawn by NS and, at the time of writing, are subject to ongoing legal action. One of them, No. 4806, is seen on a test run at Utrecht Centraal station, 24 May 2013. Thanks to Erwin Voorhaar for allowing use of his photograph.

To allow internal HSL services to continue, Nederlandse Spoorwegen operates the Amsterdam to Breda service using conventional carriages and TRAXX locomotives able to operate on most European electrification systems. Decorated in 'Fyra' livery, locomotive No. 186 114, is seen on such duties at the west end of Amsterdam Centraal station on 5 May 2012. The service has since been renamed 'Intercity Direct' to prevent confusion with the failed 'Fyra' service.

For the so-called 'Benelux' service from Amsterdam to Brussels twelve Mat '54 'Hondekop' EMUS were built capable of operating on the two DC systems the Dutch and Belgium railways. Each unit had two pantographs – one for each voltage. Seen operating under the 1,500 V DC catenary at Den Haag Holland Spoor station are these two-car sets, in September 1983.

Loco-hauled workings replaced the EMUs on the 'Benelux', until recently in the hands of Belgian Railways (NMBS) dual-voltage electric locomotives. On Saturday 7 March 2009, No. 1182 has just arrived and terminated at 's-Hertogenbosch, diverted here due to engineering work north of Roosendaal. This class 11 loco was one of a dozen built in the mid-1980s for these duties.

Another photograph of NMBS class 11 No. 1182, seen on 24 June 2009, negotiating the scissors crossover at Roosendaal station. This type of electric locomotive has now been withdrawn and class 186 TRAXX locomotives have since taken over the service.

TRAXX electric locomotive No. 186 116 on a 'Benelux' service calls at Rotterdam Centraal on 4 July 2010. Owned by Angel Trains Cargo, a UK-based leasing company, this particular loco has since been repainted in Nederlandse Spoorwegen's standard yellow livery.

Featured here is TRAXX locomotive 186 201, again owned by Angel Trains, but this time leased to Belgium Railways (NMBS) where it has been given number 2809 as an identity. It is seen in the Netherlands, at Roosendaal, on 7 July 2010, waiting for a southbound freight.

The major advantage of the TRAXX class of electric locomotive is that they can operate virtually anywhere in Europe. Another loco hired to NMBS, 2834/E 186 226, is seen in charge of a rake of Belgian coaches, arriving empty in Amsterdam Centraal station on 5 May 2012.

The line between Gouda and Alphen aan den Rijn was subject to a trial of light rail technology by Nederlandse Spoorwegen. The vehicles used were originally intended for Sweden. Here, car No. 6105 is seen arriving at its dedicated low platform at Gouda station on 24 June 2009. The light rail vehicles shared NS tracks with conventional traffic, each having different height platforms at the intermediate station. The cars were withdrawn later in 2009 and conventional EMUs now operate the line.

Valkenburg station, on the NS Maastricht to Heerlen line in Limburg province, was opened as early as 23 October 1853. The station building is now classed as a national monument. Though no longer in its original use, the structure was in superb condition on 1 July 2010. Regular steam trains from the Zuid Limburgse Stoomtrein Maatschappij preservation centre in Simpelveld still serve this station on certain summer days.

Trains from the Belgian Railway network regularly enter Nederlandse Spoorwegen territory. One location, as we have already seen, is Roosendaal, while the other is the city of Maastricht, with traffic coming into the station from the direction of Liège (Luik in Dutch). Just arrived from that direction, having propelled its train from Brussels into the station, 5 March 2009, is NMBS/SNCB electric locomotive No. 1351. Part of an order for sixty, this class of motive power was built by Alsthom between 1997 and 2001. Twenty identical locomotives were also ordered by Luxembourg Railways (CFL).

NMBS AM75 type EMUs are frequent visitors to Roosendaal, on the hourly all stations service from Antwerpen. Known locally as 'Varkensneus' (pig's nose), for obvious reasons, this batch of units, forty-four in total, were built between 1975 and 1977 for local and semi-fast passenger services. Four-car unit 817 is seen at Roosendaal, forming an evening service back to Belgium on 5 March 2009.

Deutsche Bahn's famous high-speed trains, known as ICE sets, are regular visitors to the Netherlands, running from the south of Germany via Frankfurt Airport and Köln (Cologne in English), crossing the border west of Emmerich and terminating at Amsterdam Centraal. One of the ICE 3 sets, built between period between 1997 and 2006, is seen calling at Arnhem on 18 June 2009. Unlike the earlier ICE sets, this version is a true electrical multiple-unit.

On 3 July 2010, another DB ICE 3 is seen passing Ede-Wageningen station at speed, heading for Amsterdam. Ede-Wageningen is the junction station for Ede Centrum and the single-line to Amersfoort.

Much of Nederlandse Spoorwegen's freight operations have passed to Deutsche Bahn. In full DB livery, at the interchange yard between DB and NS at Venlo, is No. 6417, seen on 15 October 2013. This locomotive had been new to NS in 1989. Ten years later it passed to Railion Benelux, then Railion Nederland, both DB subsidiaries, carrying the same number throughout.

Deutsche Bahn operates into the Nederlandse Spoorwegen station at Enschede, albeit with no physical connection between the two. A Bombardier-built Talent DMU, DB No. 643 558, arrives at Enschede on a service from Münster on 21 June 2009. The train would have entered the Netherlands just after leaving the town of Gronau, where passport and customs checks still occasionally occur. DB also operates DMU services into Heerlen, from Aachen.

Two more ex-Nederlandse Spoorwegen diesels, No. 6425 and an unidentified sister, with evidence of Railion ownership, pass through Tilburg station with a westbound oil train on 7 July 2010. A total of 120 of these locomotives were built for NS; the entire class went to NS Cargo, then on to Railion Nederland and eventually passing to DB Schenker Rail Nederland.

Another member of the former NS 6400 class, No. 6497, passes north through Dordrecht station with a trip freight on 5 July 2010. This loco is seen in full red Railion Nederland livery.

As we have already seen, the freight division of Nederlandse Spoorwegen, NS Cargo, passed to Railion Nederland in 1999. Thirty-seven NS class 1600 electric locomotives were included in the transaction. Here, on 4 May 2012, No. 1611 passes Leiden station, southbound, in full Deutsche Bahn colours.

Also owned by Railion Nederland, an ex-NS Nederlandse Spoorwegen class 1600 No. 1614, named *Schiedam*, is still in NS yellow livery, albeit with Railion identity, as it arrives at Amsterdam Centraal with an international train from Germany, 1 March 2008.

The Netherlands

Deutsche Bahn are able to operate their class 189 electric locomotives into the Dutch city of Venlo, a major junction on the NS system. One is seen sandwiched between a pair of Railion Nederland 6400 class diesels, with No. 6513 closest to the camera in the yard beside Venlo station on 1 July 2010.

German freight operator ITL Eisenbahngesellschaft have two class 186 TRAXX electric locomotives, one of which, E186 150, is seen on 5 March 2009, passing through Tilburg station, heading west. Privately owned freight operators are a common site in the Netherlands today.

Thalys, the brand name of the joint operation by the Belgian and French rail systems, operates high-speed services between Paris, Brussels and Amsterdam, with some trains also running to Köln in Germany. Based on a French TGV (Train à Grand Vitesse), set number 4534 is seen in Amsterdam, heading for Schipol Airport, Brussels and Paris, as it passes Sneevlietweg metro station on 6 July 2010.

On page 14 we saw an NS 'Hondekop' two-car EMU operating the line from Ede-Wageningen to Amersfoort service. Today that route is served by these unusual German-built Protos EMUs, operated by Connexxion, but branded as 'Valleilijn', as seen on this service, in the main station at Amersfoort, 3 July 2010.

Many of the former Nederlandse Spoorwegen rural routes are today franchised out to other operators, such as Syntus. Following financial problems, the company has, since 2012, become jointly owned by French Railways' subsidiary Keolis and a Canadian concern. Syntus operate a fleet of diesel multiple units in the south and east of the Netherlands, including the service from Dordrecht to Arnhem via Tiel. The latter station, serving a small town in Gelderland, is where a Syntus LINT DMU is meeting a terminating NS DD-AR class EMU on 8 July 2010.

Syntus also operate the Oldenzaal (Overijssel) to Zutphen (Gelderland) local service via Hengelo. On 23 June 2009, LINT DMU No. 30 is seen in the terminating platform at Oldenzaal. Electric trains continue beyond here into Germany, used by international services via Bad Bentheim.

The eastern part of Gelderland province is very rural, close to the German border. A single-line non-electrified route serves the area with its centre point being Winterswijk, where Syntus has a depot to maintain its fleet of LINT DMUs. Two are seen at that station on 3 July 2010.

In a special red livery for the Twente area of Overijssel province, Syntus DMU No. 45 is seen departing from Mariënberg on the single-line route to Almelo on 23 June 2009. The DMU would have connected with a Nederlandse Spoorwegen electric service on the busy branch to Emmen.

French-based Veolia, part of the Transdev Group, operated buses and trains in the Netherlands, particularly around Limburg Province. The company ran a fleet of Stadler 'Spurt' articulated DMUs, but also some similar EMUs. Here set No. 653, built by Stadler, is seen at the end of the branch at Kerkrade Centrum, very close to the German border, 1 July 2010. The unit will soon return through Limburg to Maastricht Randwyck. The concession to run the Limburg services has since expired and Connexxion operate these at the time of writing.

Deutsche Bahn owned Arriva operate the majority of secondary lines in the provinces of Friesland and Groningen, including the two-hourly service to Leer in Germany. However, at the time of writing, the latter service is curtailed due to a bridge problem. A fleet of Stadler 'Spurt' DMUs, both two- and three-car sets, operate these lines. A popular branch line is that to Harlingen Haven, where a two-car set is seen on 7 October 2011. Connections can be made from here to the Friesian island of Terschelling.

Several rural branches radiate from the capital of Friesland Province, Leeuwarden, including that to Harlingen (see previous picture) and to the seaside town of Stavoren. Two-car Arriva 'Spurt' DMU is seen here on 5 October 2011. The recently installed buffer stop will be noted. The previous year, a Speno rail grinding train had demolished the previous buffers at high speed, passing through an entire building before eventually coming to a halt.

To the west of the country, Arriva use Stadler electric multiple units on local routes. On 5 July 2010, EMU No. 407 is seen awaiting its next duty as it sits in a siding beside Dordrecht station.

As well as Deutsche Bahn, other companies operate freight services in the Netherlands. One of these is ACTS, who once ran several ex-British Rail class 58 locos. These have since been withdrawn and replaced by locos such as this Vossloh G1206, No. 7108. It is seen at Hengelo, a major interchange station in Overijssel Province, on 23 June 2009.

Various infrastructure companies have locomotives that operate over Dutch Railways' metals. Spitzke Spoorbouw BV, on 19 June 2009, was using this former Deutsche Reichsbahn diesel loco at Zutphen station. The loco was built in 1974 and here carries the name *Mariëlle* and 'V100-SP-004' as its identity.

The city of Rotterdam opened the first section of its Metro system in 1968, operating between Centraal Station and Zuidplein, passing under the Nieuwe Maas River in a tunnel. However, the penultimate station, Maashaven, was above street level when one of the EMUs was photographed in 1972.

Since the last photograph, the Rotterdam Metro has been considerably extended. Unit No. 5216 is seen at Schiedam station on 5 July 2010, where interchange was available with NS services.

In both the Netherlands and Belgium, the distinctions between railways and tramways can be confusing. The Dutch city of Utrecht began operating the Sneltram (fast tram) over former Nederlandse Spoorwegen metals to Nieuwegein in 1983. Two years later a branch opened to Ijsselstein, which is where Connexxion (who had the concession to operate the system) No. 5002 and a sister are heading. The four-car set is seen at Utrecht Centraal Station terminus on 3 March 2007.

The concession to operate the Utrechtse Sneltram has now passed to Qbuzz, whose livery is seen applied to set 5020 at a temporary terminus at Utrecht Centraal Station on 12 October 2013.

As a temporary measure, between 2009 and 2014 some former Vienna trams were brought in to assist in operation of the Utrechtse Sneltram system. Still in its red livery, set 4941 departs from Utrecht Centraal Station on 1 July 2010, heading for Nieuwegein Zuid. Delivery of new Spanish-built trams commenced early in 2017.

The Dutch capital city of Amsterdam opened a metro system in 1977, which has gradually expanded under the management of Gemeentelijk Vervoerbedrijf (GVB). One of the original units is seen departing from Amsterdam Zuid station on 6 July 2010. These units were finally withdrawn in 2015.

One of the newer GVB Metro units, No. 101, is seen arriving at Sneevlietweg station on 6 July 2010, on route 50. This type of train was introduced from 1997 onwards.

Route 51 on the GVB Metro system takes to the streets over conventional tramlines, albeit here on reserved tracks. Unit No. 73 approaches A. J. Ernststraat halt en route to Westwijk on 6 July 2010.

GVB Amsterdam also runs trams on route 5 over the tracks seen in the last photograph. Tram No. 917 is seen at the same spot on 6 July 2010, heading for Amstelveen Stadshart (Binnenhof). This particular class of vehicle was introduced in 1990.

The Randstad is the name given to the conurbation in Noord and Zuid Holland provinces, which includes the cities of Amsterdam, Den Haag (The Hague) and Rotterdam. Randstadrail now operates low-floor trams and conventional metro-type trains over former Nederlandse Spoorwegen lines out from Den Haag and through Rotterdam. Interchange is possible with NS at Laan van N. O. I. Station, where low-floor tram 4035 is seen arriving at its compatible platform on 24 June 2009.

Two-car Randstadrail metro set No. 5503 leads a sister unit into the conventional height platform at Laan van N. O. I. Station in Den Haag on 24 June 2009. The train is heading for its terminus at Den Haag Centraal Station.

Randstadrail set No. 5503 is coincidentally photographed again, on 5 July 2010, this time at what was then the terminus of the line at Rotterdam Hofplein. Later in that year Hofplein station was closed and the Randstadrail line was diverted into a tunnel below Rotterdam Centraal station and towards a southern extension.

The Dutch national railway museum was opened in 1954 at the former Maliebaan station in central Utrecht. Over the years the exhibition areas have expanded to both sides of the operational railway line that runs through the site. In the main hall, high up on a plinth, is former Nederlansche Rhijnspoorweg-Maatschappij (NSR) 4-4-0 express steam locomotive No. 107, built in the UK by Sharp Stewart in 1889. Seen on 8 July 2010.

On the same occasion as above, this steam locomotive in the museum at Utrecht will seem very familiar to British eyes. Built by the North British Locomotive Company in Glasgow in 1945 with a 2-10-0 wheel arrangement for the UK War Department for operation in mainland Europe following cessation of the hostilities of the Second World War, this particular locomotive was the 1,000th British-built one that crossed the Channel since 'D' Day, hence the name *Longmoor* given to No. 73755. It was later sold to Nederlandse Spoorwegen, with whom it ran until 1952 when it was stored for preservation.

Preserved steam has long been allowed to operate over Nederlandse Spoorwegen metals. In 1977, former Deutsche Bundesbahn (West German Railways) 2-6-2 No. 23 023 is seen at Rotterdam Centraal station. One of 102 such locomotives, 23 023 was constructed in 1952. In its service years with DB it would have been regularly seen in the Netherlands at such places as Venlo and Nijmegen. It is currently owned by Stoom Stichting Nederland, a railway museum in Rotterdam, but is out of use at the time of writing.

The Veluwsche Stoomtrein Maatschappij operates the former NS line between Apeldoorn and Dieren using steam trains on certain days of the year. Awaiting departure at Apeldoorn on 19 June 2009 is another ex-DB 2-6-2, No. 23 076.

The Zuid-Limburgse Stoomtrein Maatschappij (ZLSM) is a preserved railway operation based in Simpelveld, a former NS rural junction. Three lines radiate from here – one into Germany (Vetschau near Aachen), one to Kerkrade and the other to Schin op Geul, where a physical connection is made with the Dutch national rail system, enabling the ZLSM to run through to Valkenburg. Ex-DB railbuses normally operate the first two branches, but the latter requires a locomotive capable of keeping up with regular EMU service on the main line. The regular performer on these duties is former Swedish Railways 2-8-0 steam locomotive No. 1040, built in 1910 and seen at Simpelveld on 21 June 2009.

The rural line between Haaksbergen and Boekelo, near Hengelo in Overijssel Province, is now isolated from the main national network, but has been retained as a preserved railway. Various very well-presented steam locomotives are operated, with this example looking superb as it sits in the sun at Boekelo station on 21 June 2009. It is 2-6-0 tank locomotive, numbered 152 and built by Henschel in Germany in 1927.

The Stoomtram Hoorn-Medemblik, a preserved standard gauge steam tramline, or light railway, runs between the NS served station at Hoorn to the former coastal resort of Medemblik on the body of water known as the IJsselmeer. A fantastic selection of locomotives make up the line's motive power, an example being this German-built Arnold Jung 0-4-0 tank, constructed in 1908 for the gasworks in Rotterdam, now numbered 30. It is seen outside the engine shed at Hoorn – the society's headquarters – in September 1983.

Stoomtram Hoorn-Medemblik also owns several diesel locos, though they are not regularly used on passenger services. At Hoorn, again in September 1983, we see this Motorenfabrik Deutz shunter built in 1953.

Coupled to a great variety of rolling stock at Hoorn on 2 May 2012 is this former Nederlandse Spoorwegen four-wheel diesel shunter, No. 288. Built at the Centrale Werkplaats NS at Zwolle in 1938, this loco arrived at Hoorn in 2010.

Another view of Stoomtram Hoorn-Medemblik locomotive No. 30, seen during its run round manoeuvre after arriving at Medemblik – a beautiful Noord Holland town on the IJsselmeer, which is just behind the embankment seen behind the platform, 2 May 2012.

The Stoomtram Hoorn–Medemblik line also has a wonderfully restored collection of passenger rolling stock, such as this ex-Zeeuwsch-Vlaamsche Tramweg Maatschappij (ZVTM) bogie car seen at Medemblik on 2 May 2012. The ZVTM ran rural services in the Zeeuwsch-Vlanderen area of Zeeland Province, situated south of the River Schelde.

At Medemblik, the Stoomtram Hoorn–Medemblik connects with a preserved ferry to take tourists and enthusiasts along the IJsselmeer coastline to the town of Enkhuizen, where connections can be made with NS trains back to Hoorn, this forming a triangle (*driehoek* in Dutch). On 2 May 2012, the vessel, named *Friesland*, built in 1953 to serve the island of Terschelling, is seen arriving at Medemblik.

The town of Goes, on the NS line between Roosendaal and Vlissingen, in Zeeland Province, is the home of another preserved railway line, the Stoomtrein Goes-Borsele (SGB). On a non-running day in November 1977, ex-NS diesel-electric shunter No. 352, built in 1936, is seen with some historic stock at Goes, the headquarters of the line.

One of the restored steam locomotives on the Stoomtrein Goes-Borsele line, No. 3 *Bison*, brings empty stock into the SGB station at Goes on 7 July 2010. This 0-6-0T locomotive was built in 1928 by La Meuse in Liège (*Luik* in Dutch) in Belgium.

On the same occasion as the last photo, SGB loco No. 3 *Bison* is seen at its southern terminus at Hoedekenskerke, running round its train. The line extends beyond here, but is only available to diesel railbus services.

On arrival at Hoedekenskerke, passengers can find a variety of things to do and see. A couple of cafés provide refreshments, there are wonderful views over the Schelde estuary towards Belgium, and a miniature railway provides a ride of nearly a kilometre for children of all ages. On 7 July 2010, a small-scale version of an NS 600 class 0-6-0 diesel hauls a well-laden train past the extensive servicing facilities.

Belgium

Steam had officially ended on the Belgium rail system when this photograph by Tony Martens was taken of the shed at Charleroi from a passing train in the early 1970s. Four SNCB class 81 0-8-0 locomotives are seen out of use and awaiting the breaker's torch.

Built in 1928, this 0-4-0 tank locomotive was constructed by La Meuse in Belgium for SNCB/NMBS – the national railway system in the country. After a long service, the small shunter was preserved and placed on a plinth, where it is seen, at Namur station, in autumn 1997. At the time, the station was undergoing modernisation and rebuilding and shortly after the loco was removed into storage.

Belgium

Very few Trans Europe Express (TEE) diesel multiple units were built, with only the Swiss and Dutch rail systems ordering them. As suggested by the name, they were used on long distance services such as the 'Edelweiss' between Amsterdam and Zurich, but there were shorter workings two. The units consisted of only four vehicles, one of which was a motor luggage van, seen to the fore in this photograph taken by Tony Martens at Brussels Midi/Zuid in the very early 1970s. All were withdrawn in 1974 and were sold to a Canadian operator a few years later.

SNCF, the state operator of French Railways has long operated into Brussels, in more recent years using their prestigious TGV (Train à Grand Vitesse or High Speed Train) sets, such as No. 4511, seen at Brussels Midi/Zuid in March 1995, not long after entering service.

Eurostar commenced operations to Brussels from London Waterloo in November 1994, via the Channel Tunnel. Improvements over the years saw the opening of the High Speed 1 route in England, diversion of the service into St Pancras, and the construction of a high-speed route between Lille and Brussels. The latter has its northern end near the town of Halle and Eurostar services are obliged to use conventional metals for the last few kilometres into Brussels. On this section, passing Ruisbroek station, is a London bound service, a midday departure from Brussels, led by half-set No. 3107 on 9 October 2012.

The Amsterdam/Köln–Brussels–Paris high-speed service is today operated by Thalys, a jointly owned business, with SNCF having the majority shareholding. Services are operated by TGV sets painted in the appropriate colours. On 9 October 2012, a northbound Thalys overtakes a NMBS local EMU service calling at Ruisbroek.

Belgium

Over the years the Belgian rail network has seen a variety of diesel shunting locomotives for work in freight yards and for station pilot duties. The NMBS/SNCB class 83 0-6-0 diesel hydraulics were introduced in 1956, a total of twenty-five being constructed by Cockerill in Belgium. Here is No. 8325, seen in the early 1970s, shunting stock at Gent Sint Pieters station. All were withdrawn by 1994. Photograph by Tony Martens.

The NMBS class 84 diesel hydraulic shunting locos were introduced into service between 1955 and 1962, with seventy being received in all. The class was finally withdrawn in 2005. Long before that, on a rainy day in September 1983, No. 8437 is seen busying itself in the marshalling yards in the outskirts of Oostende.

NMBS certainly liked their diesel hydraulic 0-6-0 shunting locomotives, as the company took delivery of well over 150 of the outwardly identical classes 73, 74 and 82. One of the latter, No. 8247, is seen taking charge of some empty coaching stock at Antwerpen Centraal station in September 1983.

On 22 January 1994, Richard Huggins photographed NMBS class 73 No. 7366 (unofficially named *Bravo*) at Mol station on the Antwerpen to Neerpelt and Hasselt route. All the class 73, 74 and 82 locomotives had been withdrawn by the early years of the twenty-first century.

Running into Antwerpen Centraal station in September 1983 is NMBS class 59 diesel locomotive No. 5902. The class 59 was a mixed traffic locomotive type, built by Cockerill in 1954 and 1955. A total of fifty-five were constructed and all had been withdrawn by 1988. The walls of Antwerpen Zoo, adjacent to Centraal station, can be seen in the background.

Cockerill built ninety-three class 51 diesel-electric Co-Co locomotives for NMBS between 1961 and 1963. A fine example of the type is No. 5134 hauling a rake of decidedly ancient-looking passenger stock (including a 'birdcage' fitted brake compartment) into Gent Sint Pieters station in September 1983. All the class 51 locos have been withdrawn, though several are preserved.

The NMBS class 62 and 63 Bo-Bo locomotives were in normal service between 1961 and 2003, in charge of a variety of traffic. On a showery day in September 1983, No. 6210 is seen at Gent Sint Pieters station with a local train heading towards the coast.

NMBS class 62 locomotive No. 6291 is seen at Neerpelt, the terminus of the non-electrified line from Mol, on 22 January 1994. The line has since 2014 been extended towards the Dutch border to the town of Hamont. Today the service is operated by class 41 diesel multiple units. Several class 62 locomotives remain in service with Infrabel, who maintain the tracks of which Belgian trains operate. Thanks to Richard Huggins for this photograph.

Former NMBS class 62 locomotives 6237 and 6283, still in their former colours, are seen with Infrabel in the sidings at Lier in Antwerpen Province, on 30 June 2010.

The Belgian class 60 Bo-Bo locomotives were built by Cockerill in the first half of the 1960s. No. 6007 had been delivered as No. 210 077 and given that number once again when it was photographed by Richard Huggins on a railtour visiting the Budel Zinc Works branch very close to the Dutch border near to Hamont on 22 January 1994.

The modern SNCB diesel locomotive in use today is the class 77 Bo-Bo, with Voith hydraulic transmission. Used for shunting and freight duties, the class of 170 locos was built between 1999 and 2005. Running light through the impressive Liège Guillemins station is No. 7750 on 27 April 2013.

NMBS class 77 No. 7778 and an unidentified sister are in charge of an oil train as they pass through Antwerpen-Luchtbal station near the city's docks, on 29 September 2010.

Belgium

Ubiquitous throughout Belgium are the MS50/AM50 ('Automotrice 1950' in French) type of electric multiple units, though there are numerous variations of these two-car sets. One of the 1950-built units, No. 017, seen in its original livery, arrives at Antwerpen Centraal in September 1983. It is accompanying a 'Varkensneus' (pig's nose) EMU in its original livery.

NMBS EMU No. 528 runs into Gent Sint Pieters station in September 1983. The original yellow stripes on the front of these units was deemed to be insufficient to be easily seen by track workers, hence the painting of the communicating door in that colour, as seen here. Wooden seats were originally fitted in this type of unit when used on Brussels suburban services.

Unit No. 255, built in the 1960s, is seen in its red colour scheme, standing under the modernistic overall roof of Liège Guillemins station on 27 July 2008.

The coastal town of Knokke, close to the Dutch border, lies at the end of a short branch off the main Brugge to Oostende line. On 27 June 2009, EMU No. 676 is seen forming the shuttle to Brugge (Bruges as the Wallonians and British insist on calling it).

Modernised unit No. 748, resplendent in the latest NMBS livery, calls at Lot between Halle and Brussels Midi/Zuid on a northbound suburban working on 26 April 2012.

In a similar colour scheme, EMU No. 992, lettered for 'CitiRail' duties, forms a local service at Charleroi Sud (the main station serving that city) on 28 February 2008.

Eight of the original Type 1935 electric multiple units built for NMBS were later converted to postal units and therefore experienced a long life. One of them, No. 956, rests at Oostende station in September 1983. All have since been withdrawn.

Introduced between 1975 and 1977, the MS75 class of four-car EMU were soon nicknamed 'Varkensneus' (pig's nose) for obvious reasons. Delivered in insipid orange and grey colours, they were intended for semi-fast services. On such a duty, in September 1983, No. 840 awaits departure at Oostende.

The MS75 class soon received a dark red livery, as displayed on unit No. 809, at Antwerpen Centraal station on 4 March 2007.

NMBS uses the MS75 class of EMU on the local service from Antwerpen Centraal to Roosendaal, the first station over the border in the Netherlands. On such a duty is No. 811, seen departing from Antwerpen Dam station northbound on 18 September 2010.

The Dutch word for goggles is *Duikbril* and it doesn't come as any surprise that that has become the nickname for the MS86 class of NMBS two-car EMU. Built between 1986 and 1991, the units are mainly used on local services. On such a duty, set No. 940 arrives at Haacht on the Mechelen to Leuven line on 4 March 2011.

Two NMBS class MS86 EMU sets, led by No. 933, arrive at Antwerpen Berchem station on a sunny but cold 3 March 2008.

Belgium

Originally built as two-car sets, the class MS80 (and the following MS82 and MS83) EMUs were delivered in the early 1980s. Most were later converted to three cars and are today used on semi-fast services, such as the line terminating at De Panne, where connections can be made with the southern end of the coastal tramway. Unit No. 419, partly graffitied, sits in De Panne (Adinkerke) station on 30 June 2009.

Similar unit 325 departs from Lier on 25 April 2013, heading for either Aarschot or Turnhout.

Nicknamed *Deense Neus* (Danish Nose) after similar-looking units in Denmark, the NMBS class MS96 of EMU will never win any prizes for their looks! However, these three-car sets are air conditioned, very comfortable, and used on long distance services, including those into Lille in France and Luxembourg. Built in 1996, unit No. 479 is seen at Antwerpen Centraal station on 29 February 2008.

Antwerpen Centraal station was originally a terminal station, situated above street level. Recent rebuilding has seen it rebuilt to become a through station, with trains for the north using the deep level platforms and new tunnels, while terminating trains from the south can still use some of the original platforms and those on the new intermediate level. The magnificent features of the station have been beautifully restored, as seen by this part of the original station on 2 March 2008.

Belgium

The newest EMUs for NMBS are of the MS08 class, introduced during the second decade of the twenty-first century, for local and semi-fast services. Arriving at Hove, on the line towards Brussels, between Antwerpen and Mechelen, on 2 October 2014, is three-car unit No. 08121.

SNCB MS08 class EMU No. 08511 is seen on a semi-fast duty at Libramont station, on the main line towards Luxembourg, on 27 April 2014. Over 300 of these sets have now been delivered.

SNCB purchased fifty-six single-car diesel units for local services over non-electrified lines in Belgium. The long branch to Couvin in Namur Province is still diesel operated and, in the early 1970s, car No. 4509 is seen at Charleroi Sud station on such a duty. Photograph by Tony Martens.

Railcar No. 4405 is approaching Gent Sint Pieters station on a service from Geraardsbergen, passing the junction with the line from Antwerpen via Gent Dampoort in September 1983. All these units have since been withdrawn, though some have been preserved.

Ninety-six two-car diesel multiple units have been delivered to NMBS for non-electrified routes. Delivered between 2000 and 2002, they have replaced all the previous DMUs and several loco-hauled services. Several services out of Gent are still diesel-operated, including those to Geraardsbergen, Ronse/Renaix and Eeklo. On a working to the latter destination, set No. 4184 is seen at Gent Sint Pieters station on 29 June 2009.

DMU No. 4178 is getting ready for its journey back to Antwerpen Centraal at its terminus at Neerpelt on 3 March 2010. The service has since been extended to Hamont.

A former Belgian manufacturer, Baume & Marpent, built the class 120 electric locomotives of NMBS, a batch of just three locomotives, in 1949. Originally numbered 120 001 etc., they received new identities as 2801-2 in 1975. Numerically the first of the trio, No. 2801 is seen in the loco sidings at Oostende station, alongside Co-Co electric No. 2014 in September 1983.

A total of fifty class 22 Bo-Bo electric locomotives entered service with NMBS/SNCB in 1954. They operated throughout the country and into Luxembourg. Withdrawal began in 2002 and the entire class had vanished by 2009. No. 2219 is seen taking a break in the sidings at Brussels Midi/Zuid, along with station pilot No. 8062 in September 1983.

Belgium

The class 23 locomotives were also used on international services and No. 2351 is undertaking such a duty at Brussels Midi/Zuid in September 1983, looking decidedly antique compared to the SNCF TGV in the background. Introduced in 1955, the class finally vanished in 2012.

The year 1964 saw the introduction of the prototype class 26 NMBS electric locomotives, but the other thirty-four in the batch were received in the late 1960s and early 1970s. No. 2610 is in charge of an eastbound freight, probably from the port of Zeebrugge, passing through Gent Sint Pieters station on 29 June 2009. Two years later, the class was withdrawn.

Clearly displaying its French design and similarity to the CC40100 locomotives of SNCF, NMBS No. 1805 has just uncoupled from its train at Oostende in September 1983. Only six of these locos were operated by Belgian Railways, built during 1973 and 1974 by Alsthom; all had been withdrawn by 1999.

The class 20 was a powerful-looking Co-Co electric locomotive introduced in the mid-1970s. A total of twenty-five were built. In its original green livery, No. 2014 is seen on arrival at Oostende in September 1983. The class went out of service in 2013.

Belgium

NMBS later repainted the class 20 locomotives into its standard blue colour scheme, seen applied to No. 2003 as it passes through Arlon station heading light engine towards Luxembourg in 1991.

Another class 20, No. 2002, is seen on a southbound container train from Antwerpen Docks about to pass through Antwerpen Berchem station on 3 March 2008.

All the NMBS electric locomotive classes we have seen so far have been withdrawn. However, the class 27 mixed traffic Bo-Bo remains in service, still operating a variety of traffic. Introduced during the early 1980s, No. 2710 was almost new when photographed at Oostende on September 1983.

A total of sixty class 27 locomotives were built for NMBS, so the class can frequently be seen all over Belgium. These locos can operate in push-pull mode, as illustrated by this photograph of No. 2706 propelling a heavily graffitied semi-fast service out of Mechelen Nekkerspoel station on 1 October 2015.

During the evening of 6 March 2009, NMBS No. 2737 prepares to propel a set of double-deck coaching stock out of the high-level platforms of Antwerpen Centraal station.

Another product of the 1980s, the class 21 is very similar to the class 27 and used on the same types of duties. No. 2135 has just arrived at the Level 2 terminating platforms at Antwerpen Centraal, on the rear of an express on 24 June 2009.

One of sixty class 21 electric locomotives, No. 2140 is seen on the rear of a lengthy local train of push-pull stock calling at Haacht on 4 June 2013. Although a considerable distance from the town of the same name, the Haacht Brewery and its splendid tap room are only a few yards away.

Introduced during 1986, the NMBS class 12 Bo-Bo dual-voltage electric locomotives are capable of running into Northern France. One of only twelve built, No. 1206 is seen passing a wall of graffiti beside Antwerpen Berchem station on 3 March 2008.

The purchase by NMBS of the class 13 batch of modern electric locomotives, totally sixty, meant the demise of many earlier electric classes. Again, these are capable of operating on the Belgian 3,000 volt DC system and 25KV AC. They were built between 1997 and 2001, for mixed traffic duties. Operating a heavy freight is No. 1306 and an unidentified sister, seen on 4 October 2013, approaching Haacht station. The third loco in the consist, not under power, is an identical CFL class 3000.

The presence of a hill behind the locomotive in this photograph tells us that we are in Wallonia, the French-speaking part of Belgium. The location is Libramont, on the main Brussels to Luxembourg route. Class 13 No. 1349 is attached to a set of double-deck stock forming a semi-fast service on 27 April 2013.

NMBS No. 2811, a.k.a. E186 283, is a Bombardier TRAXX Bo-Bo electric locomotive capable of operating of operating under a variety of voltage systems. Rapidly becoming the standard loco in Western Europe, over forty are now in Belgian service. This one is seen on a westbound freight at Lier on 25 April 2014.

The newest electric locos for NMBS are of class 18 and 19, entering service between 2009 and 2012. Built by Siemens, a total of 120 were ordered, with the ability to operate under 1,500 Volts DC, 3,000 Volts DC and 25 KV AC overhead line regimes. On 26 April 2013, No. 1844 is in charge of a double-deck passenger service at Tongeren, Belgium's oldest town.

Not all freight traffic in Belgium is operated by the state-owned railway company. Several private companies have entered the fray. Many of these use the class 66 diesels very familiar to British eyes. Here, on 4 March 2011, No. 29002 – hired to Crossrail from a Luxembourg leasing company – approaches Haacht westbound.

Deutsche Bahn Nederland also takes charge of some freight in Belgium. Here, at Hove, in the south Antwerpen suburbs, ex-Nederlandse Spoorwegen Bo-Bo diesel No. 6519 heads north with a mixed freight on 1 October 2015. Hove station is now unstaffed, but the buildings have been converted into an excellent bar.

Brussels has an extensive Metro system today. Much of the underground portion was constructed as a tramway, described as 'Pre-Metro', which was later changed to full Metro standards. At the time of writing, there are two types of train in use, though some new stock is on order. On 16 September 2010, one of the older units, with car 120 closest to the camera, is seen at Erasmus station, the western terminus of Line 5.

One of the more modern sets of Brussels Metro stock, with car 6141 at the rear, waits to depart from Stokkel, at the eastern end of Line 1, again on 16 September 2010.

Several preserved railways operate in Belgium. Perhaps one of the most famous is the Chemin de Fer à vapeur des Trois Vallées based on the town of Mariembourg in Namur Province. It is a standard gauge line running to Treignes, where 0-8-0T No. AD07, built by La Meuse in 1942, stands with a train around 1984. Photograph by Tony Martens.

Also photographed by Tony Martens during the same visit is this tiny Cockerill 0-4-0 vertical boilered tank locomotive DG22, seen outside the shed at Mariembourg. It was built in 1913.

The Stoomcentrum Maldegem is a preserved steam centre based at Maldegem in Oost Vlanderen (East Flanders) Province. A short narrow gauge line is in use, but the main operation is the former NMBS line to Eeklo, where connections can be made for Gent and beyond. On 19 September 2010, loco No. TKh 5387, an 0-6-0T built in 1959 for a cement works in Poland, waits for departure at Maldegem.

On the same occasion, ex-NMBS railcar No. 4403 approaches the level crossing at Maldegem as it departs for Eeklo.

An unusual tourist operation is provided by the 'Railbike' system based on the Ardennes village of Falaën, from where one can pedal along a former Belgian Railways line to either Warnant or Maredsous. In 2001, on the latter section, one of the four-seat vehicles is seen in action, with the author hard at work on the left.

An extensive metre-gauge system, called the Vicinal in French or Buurtspoorweg in Flemish, once operated throughout Belgium. A cross between a conventional tramway and a light railway, most of the network has long closed, though parts became the coastal tramway and the Charleroi tram system. In the more rural parts, steam locos were employed as motive power, such as this 1915-built example seen in the tram museum in Antwerpen on 18 September 2010.

In the Ardennes, one of the more rural Vicinal lines is now a preserved line, running from Pont d'Érizée, close to where the depot is situated. Services are normally diesel operated, but steam engines feature on special occasions. Tony Martens was fortunate enough to visit on one of these and found 0-6-0T *La Scarpe* in steam. This loco was actually from France, where it operated similar services in the north of that country.

The depot on the Pont d'Érizée line, correctly called Le Tramway Touristique de L'Aisne, is served by a halt named Blier, where, in 1997, diesel car AR 133 and a trailer are seen. Such trains were a common site in the sparsely populated areas of Belgium, the diesels often being used to haul freight and mixed trains. A different operation also runs an intensive service using similar trains, conveying tourists to the caves at Han-sur-Lesse.

Luxembourg

The Société Nationale des Chemins de Fer Luxembourgeois, henceforth referred to as CFL, operates a considerable network within the small country. Perhaps the most notable electric locomotives of recent years were those numbered 3601 to 3620. These centre-cab machines were based on the French Railways (SNCF) 12000 class. They were used on a variety of duties, both passenger and freight. Number 3603 is seen at Luxembourg City's principal station in May 2001, on a four-car passenger duty. Behind, on an international service is SNCF electric locomotive number 15010. All the CFL 3600 class were withdrawn by 2005, but some of the SNCF 15000 locos remain in service at the time of writing.

CFL's 1800 class of diesel locomotive is to the same design as the Belgian Railways class 55. A total of twenty were ordered by CFL, being delivered in the early 1960s. Originally mixed traffic locos, most have since been withdrawn. Number 1820 is seen in the southern outskirts of Luxembourg City in May 2001, on what appears to be a train of waste material.

CFL received six class 2100 single-car diesel multiple unit cars, for local and branch line services. Number 2106 waits in the small bay platform at Noertzange, on the line through Bettembourg towards France. In May 2001 the unit is ready to depart for the former mining town of Rumelange, in the very south of the country. These units did not last very long with CFL, despite being new in 2000, the entire batch being sold to SNCF.

At the end of the single-track electrified Rumelange branch, diesel unit 2106 has just arrived in the passenger platform with the service from Noertzange, again in May 2001. Meanwhile 900 class diesel locomotive number 909 waits for clearance to head north with a freight. Like the DMU, many of this class were sold for further service to SNCF.

The most northerly station on the CFL system is a Troisvierges, though the line continues on into Belgium, towards the city of Liège. On 15 August 2014, two trains are seen in the platforms here, both having just made the journey of an hour or so from Gare Centrale in Luxembourg City. On the right is electrical multiple unit number 2020, one of a batch of twenty-two such two-car units delivered to CFL in the early 1990s. Electric loco number 4002 is at the rear of a four-car double-deck push-pull set awaiting departure time. This locomotive is one of twenty owned by CFL, a variant of the Bombardier TRAXX design, capable of running into the three countries bordering Luxembourg.

Another member of the CFL class 4000, numerically the first, number 4001, stands in platform 9B at Gare Centrale in Luxembourg City on 18 August 2014. New ten years or so earlier, like many of the class it carries adverts, these praising the glories of one hundred years of Luxembourg Red Cross. It will shortly depart for Rodange, close to the French border.

Two Deutsche Bahn (DB) diesel multiple units were used by CFL to operate the Luxembourg City to Trier (Germany) via Wasserbillig route. Painted in DB colours, though with CFL markings, two-car unit number 628 506 stands in Luxembourg Gare Centrale on 15 August 2014. This DMU, together with sister unit 628 505, was returned to DB later in the same year. The line through to Trier is now electrified and CFL 4000 class locomotives usually handle the service today.

Identical to the Belgian Railways class 13 electrics, CFL's twenty class 3000 locomotives are a common sight throughout Luxembourg. Delivered between 1998 and 2001, they are used on a variety of traffic, including into Belgium. In May 2001, an example of the class, number 3009 is seen at Gare Central in Luxembourg City, on a four-coach local service.

Société Nationale des Chemins de Fer Belges (SNCB) operates regular services from Brussels and the Wallonian area of Belgium into the city of Luxembourg, using either EMUs or the class 13 electric locomotives. Introduced from 1997 until 2001, a total of sixty were produced for SNCB/NMBS. An example of the class, number 1350, is seen in Gare Central, Luxembourg City, awaiting an international service from faraway Switzerland, which it will haul to Brussels on 15 August 2014.

SNCB/NMBS class 20 electric locos were capable of running into Luxembourg on services to and from Brussels. These Co-Co machines were built between 1975 and 1977, but, despite their young age, all have now been withdrawn. Number 2009 is seen entering Gare Central, Luxembourg City, in May 2001, passing electrical multiple unit number 2002.

French Railways (Société Nationale des Chemins de Fer Français – SNCF) operate regular services into Luxembourg City, mainly using electrical multiple units, on the services towards Metz and Nancy. Dual-voltage electric locomotives can also be found, mainly on international trains. One such loco, SNCF number 126163, is seen on 15 August 2014 in charge of a rake of Belgian coaching stock, plus a Swiss Railways first class car next to the engine.

SNCF's prestigious TGV (Train à Grande Vitesse) high-speed trains are frequent visitors from Paris Gare de l'Est. One of the earlier sets, SNCF number 536, is seen on arrival at Gare Central on 15 August 2014, adding even more variety to the interesting rolling stock to be found in the Grand Duchy of Luxembourg.